THE
Romance
OF
SEX

SPECIAL DAYS & NIGHTS FOR LOVERS

PARKER PUBLISHING COMPANY
West Nyack, New York 10994

Library of Congress Cataloging-in-Publication Data

Block, Joel D.
    The romance of sex : special days and nights for lovers / Joel D. Block
        p.   cm.
    ISBN 0-13-644635-3
    1. Sex—Miscellaneous.   2. Love—Miscellaneous.   3. Man-woman relationships—
Miscellaneous.   I. Title.
HQ21.B725   1998
306.7—dc21   97-36534
                                                                            CIP

Printed in the United States of America

10 9 8 7 6 5 4 3 2 1

ISBN   0-13-644635-3

ATTENTION: CORPORATIONS AND SCHOOLS

Parker books are available at quantity discounts with bulk purchase for educational, business, or sales promotional use. For information, please write to: Prentice Hall Special Sales, 240 Frisch Court, Paramus, New Jersey 07652. Please supply: title of book, ISBN, quantity, how the book will be used, date needed.

PARKER PUBLISHING COMPANY
West Nyack, NY 10994

A Simon & Schuster Company

On the World Wide Web at http://www.phdirect.com

Prentice Hall International (UK) Limited, *London*
Prentice Hall of Australia Pty. Limited, *Sydney*
Prentice Hall Canada, Inc., *Toronto*
Prentice Hall Hispanoamericana, S.A., *Mexico*
Prentice Hall of India Private Limited, *New Delhi*
Prentice Hall of Japan, Inc., *Tokyo*
Simon & Schuster Asia Pte. Ltd., *Singapore*
Editora Prentice Hall do Brasil, Ltda., *Rio de Janeiro*

Introduction

$\mathcal{E}$ach season, each month, holds special days and nights for lovers.
A shared, steamy bubblebath takes the chill off a cold winter's night;
a walk in the spring rain gives lovers an opportunity to admire Nature
poised to blossom; a skinny-dip in a quiet lake captures the magic of a
midsummer's night; and an evening by the fire in late autumn fans flames
of desire to last the rest of the year.

Romance and sex are the perfect blend of the ethereal and the real.
Romance is the sighing and staring, the exquisite pain you feel when you
haven't seen your lover in a day, the bubbling over with joy you feel when you
hear that wonderful voice again. You are overwhelmed with how great the day
looks, how terrific the world is, how much there is to do and experience—

alone and together. Anything and everything reminds you of the person who thrills you to the core of your being.

Sex is the physical manifestation of those feelings. When you feel so strongly about another person, you have to touch—you want to get beyond the meanings that words give to our passion and meld into the one you love.

Either romance or sex can be taken separately, but when you put them together, you have a combustible and delirious combination of ingredients.

This little book is an invitation to discover and explore the rich realm of romantic lovemaking. It is a gift you give to yourself as well as to another— a new opportunity to experience the ecstasy you feel at the touch of a hand or the whisper in your ear. Let passion reign, month after month, year after year.

January

To welcome the year with excitement and passion, start with a new commitment to each other and to the pleasure you can share together.

What can you do to add adventure and delight to your sexual relationship?

What can you do to begin the year with a richer, fuller, more intensely pleasurable connection to your partner?

Add romance to your life and watch your relationship go from black and white to color. Just as a magician might pull a pristine, white dove from his hat, so you can create a mood, a moment, anytime, anywhere to thrill your lover.

The beginning of a year holds so much potential for lovers. You can decide to hold each other more, to talk more, to make love in the bathtub for the first time or stay up all night on New Year's Eve just holding hands.

Romance

It's possible that the romance that took off like a rocket when you first met is a little chilled from its long winter nap. But you can wake it up . . .

One. ***Empathize.*** If you're a romantic, you can put yourself in your partner's place. You can see and feel the world as your lover does. Empathy lets you personalize the words and gestures of love, to give what your partner desires rather than what it pleases you to give.

Two. ***Be adventurous.*** If you want to duplicate the feeling of falling in love, go white-water rafting together. Climb a mountain. Travel to foreign countries. Explore New York City on the subway.

Three. **Be sexually adventurous, too.** Try something you've never done before with anyone else. Kiss with your eyes open; embrace naked on the den rug under the piano. Add variety to your lovemaking and you'll want to make love more often.

Four. **Show physical affection.** Kisses and caresses are potent gestures. Touch gently, roughly, teasingly, meaningfully.

Five. **Do something romantic every day.** Say, "I love you." Water the plants even if it isn't your turn. Go a few blocks out of your way to pick up your lover's favorite flavor of ice cream.

Desire

*W*hen you want to, that's desire. It's the erotic urge that precedes arousal. It feels urgent, intense—as though there were a freight train right behind you. You may both feel the same desire all the time at the start of your relationship, but usually, after a while, you lose the rhythm you established together. When this happens—and it will—just go with the flow. Everything (even romance) finds its own level.

Sometimes, you feel deeply but just don't know how to express what's going on inside. Having the feelings is paramount—sharing is essential. The key to opening new doors is wanting to . . .

Tips for Handling Desire

One. **Accept that you'll get out of sync every once in a while.** Don't take it personally. Eventually, you'll get back on track.

Two. **Be more attentive to your partner's needs when you do make love.** When the reluctant partner is in the mood, make sex sizzling. Great sex once a week is better than lackluster lovemaking three times a week.

Three. **If one of you always wants more and one always wants less, accept your differences.** You're different people, so you have different needs. This is just the way you are—like your signature, it's part of your personality.

Four. **If you're the less interested partner, don't automatically say no.** Say, "maybe," as in maybe you'll change your mind in a few hours. Go ahead and touch nonsexually. Maybe later in the evening, you'll be in the mood.

JOYBREAK: STOP WORRYING AND JUST . . . ENJOY

A joybreak is the antidote to those stresses that can sap the joy from life. They are brief interludes for you to explore pleasure and romance.

For example,

♥ soften the lights, put on some music, take off your clothes, and dance slowly together.

♥ take a candlelit bubblebath.

♥ deliver a rose to your partner at work.

♥ have breakfast in bed.

♥ make plans for a getaway weekend and just enjoy the planning.

Joybreak: Sweet Sanctuary

The holidays may be over and the presents put away, but now is the time to discover that what you really want and crave is each other.

Make your home a peaceful refuge from the madding crowd—turn off the phone, put Sinatra on the CD-player. On this perfect night, you two are the stars and the moon—the entire universe.

Do a crossword puzzle lying side by side on the floor. Open the champagne, sip from each other's glass, and nibble a little on fingers and toes. Feel the warmth coming off your lover as you embrace carefully, tenderly, making it last for as long as you can hold your breaths.

Is it getting late already? Who cares? The night is young. Make love until the sun comes up.

February

$\mathscr{B}$aby, it's cold outside. The bone-chilling weather, the long, dark days drive you indoors, so that you can spend more time alone together. You are dressed in layers that can be peeled off like Scheherazade's veils.

In the bleakest cold, you find each other's warmth. Not just the warmth of breath on your skin, but the excitement in your lover's eyes, the delight in her voice when she whispers in your ear. Just what you want is to come in from a walk in the snow, have him pull off one of your gloves and put your cold fingers to his lips. Instantly, the feeling rushes back, and spreads like fire across your skin. Now, you're both warm enough.

Secrets. You can tell her things you wouldn't dream of confiding to anyone else. What your hopes and fears are, how you were so self-conscious as a teenager, how you love to be touched right behind your knees. It's terrifying, at first, to spill the beans, but it feels so good after you've been brave enough to share.

Sharing Secrets

"I wanted her to *know* me—really know everything," Jeff said. "It was such a relief when she not only listened, but understood."

"I wanted him to feel special," Maggi explained, "but more than that, I wanted him to know how similar my own fantasies were to his. We're all much more like each other than not—it's the subtle differences that attract us and make us fall so deeply for one another."

Mutual sharing of secrets can open channels of communication, help to heal past hurts, and expand your lovemaking to include all your hidden desires.

One. **Say what you really mean.** Don't beat around the bush. Let your feelings out of the box you've kept them in.

Two. **Don't be embarrassed.** Maybe you've always dreamed about putting her on a pedestal and kissing her feet; maybe she's always wanted you to blindfold her and drive her to a secluded spot in the woods. Your fantasies and desires make you interesting, not strange.

Three. **If he won't talk first, you open up the conversation.** Say it jokingly, or thoughtfully—put it out on the table and don't ask for approval. Just do it. This will encourage an exchange of wish lists between you.

Four. **Give it more than one try.** Sharing can be awkward at the beginning, but that's what building this excitement is all about. You feel tense; you feel vulnerable—that's fine. It means you care enough to share the very best of yourself.

Joybreak: A Valentine's Day Surprise

Hearts and flowers get boring year after year. But suppose you drew a heart on your lover with chocolate sauce and ate it off? Suppose you covered the entire bedroom floor with flowers and lay down on them together?

Do something lovely together to say that you are valentines now and forever. The sexual part will take care of itself—think first about what comes before and the glow that comes after.

$\mathscr{L}oveplay$

"Loveplay" is a warm-up for sex. Anytime is great for loveplay—it can go on throughout the day and night. It can be hot as a summer sun, or extremely distant—when you offer just a hint of interest in your lover. You don't even have to touch—a lot of what goes on prior to igniting is getting ready to strike the match.

Hot Loveplay Tips

One. **Remember that sex begins in the brain.** Start thinking about lovemaking hours in advance and share your thoughts. Quick calls and brief notes can be powerful erotic stimulants.

Two. **Pay attention to romantic details.** Set the stage for love: make sure the room is comfortable, the lighting just right, and put some sultry music on the stereo.

Three. **Go slow.** Begin by kissing and caressing delicately, like humming birds lighting down, then glancing off.

Four. **Experiment with varied touch.** Try "spiders' legs," a French love game, where only the fingertips and pads touch your lover's body hair. Try "spring butterfly," a Chinese game that uses the point of a dry paintbrush. With your lover's eyes closed, you can skip the brush across the body, landing lightly here and there to work your lover into a frenzy of expectation.

Five. **Experiment with different rhythms.** Get your partner excited, then back off. By teasing, you increase the level of arousal.

Afterplay

"*A*fterplay" is what you do when your passion is spent and you are lying together cuddling, caressing and sharing quiet thoughts. This can be the most intimate part of your lovemaking. People are more vulnerable to each other after sex than they are at any other time, which means that tender and affectionate afterplay can strengthen your romantic attachment.

Take advantage of those moments to stay close, whisper secrets, and inhale each other's essence. The two of you will glow.

Hints for Glowing Afterplay

One. **Express sexual feelings and thoughts you haven't yet shared.** It's nice to talk about what happened between you—not making judgments, but just saying how great certain moments were. Being playful and accepting may encourage your partner to share, too.

Two. **Laugh together.** Share a private joke.

Three. **Cuddle and caress for five minutes.** Fifteen is even better.

Four. **Say "I love you."** The words have more meaning at this special time.

March

$\mathcal{Y}$ou can feel spring coming. Your heart is tentative. The seasons are like romance itself—there is a gentle ebb and flow to your feelings as there is to the permutations of Mother Nature. Just because one day is icy doesn't mean you have to give up. Things are moving under the surface—just as they are in your relationship. You may have a silly, euphoric rush one day just seeing him turn the corner, but then another day, watching him play with the kids, you feel a soulful, relentless pull like the tides, deep inside you.

If romance has been a little slow getting to you lately, don't worry about it. The sun comes out and warms the earth as well as your hearts. And then, one day when you wake up and look at each other, you are both in bloom.

There's no better way to express how you feel than kissing the one you care about. Kisses can be casual, fun, erotic, intense, quick as a tap on the nose or long and involved and leading . . . who knows where. The old tradition of pressing lip to lip is symbolic of matching breaths—joining together at the very source of life.

Kissing

There can be no sexier interchange between two lovers than an inticing, spicy, lingering kiss. It is usually the first intimate contact with a new lover, and can be the rejuvenation of sex with an old lover. A kiss leads the way to knowing each other really well.

Prolonged, passionate kissing is very arousing. You can tell a lot about a person by the way they kiss. Try it and see.

Essential Kissing Tips

One. **Tease with your lips.** With mouth slightly open, lips firm but not rigid, begin the kiss in a light, tantalizing way.

Two. **After touching lips softly, pull away.** Lightly lick or suck your partner's lips. Then kiss again.

Three. **Vary the pace and style of your kissing.** You can be fast, slow, urgent, melting—see what variety you can create together.

Four. **Taste the tangible pleasures of a French kiss.** Use your tongue to explore your partner's mouth, but lightly. Run it over his lips, teeth, tongue, and the recessed areas inside the mouth. With the tip of your tongue, trace the inside of your lover's lips and tongue. Thrust your tongue lightly and quickly in and out of your partner's mouth. Enjoy each other thoroughly.

JOYBREAK: BEWARE THE IDES OF MARCH

Maybe you've gotten a little rusty playing with each other's emotions. Maybe it's time to shake up your relationship. The Ides of March are a perfect holiday to experiment with new methods of arousing one another's thoughts, emotions, and bodies. Try an aphrodisiac cocktail and drink it out of long-stemmed goblets, drawing down the moon to witness your passion.

Will charms and potions turn you on? Wanting makes it so. Give it a try and see.

A Persian Recipe for
Increasing Your Husband's Love

Combine cloves, cinnamon, cardamom and rose water in a pot and throw in your husband's shirt as well as a piece of paper with his name and that of four angels written on it. Heat it on the stove and read a chapter of the Koran backwards seven times. When the mixture boils, legend suggests, your husband's love for you will heat up.

Aphrodisiacs

An aphrodisiac makes you want to . . . and then helps you perform. The word is derived from the name of the Greek goddess of love and beauty, Aphrodite. Throughout history, people have believed in the erotic power of certain foods, drink, or herbs and other natural substances, some of which are actually poisonous (like the root of the mandrake, a plant in the deadly nightshade family).

Other substances reputed over the centuries to aide arousal include oysters, ginseng, powdered rhino horn, cocaine, alcohol, asparagus, pomegranates, French baguettes, and figs. Have any of these ever been proven to increase libido or potency? No. But they're fun to experiment with and may add spice to your romantic encounters.

No chemical substance yet discovered can rival *love* as an aphrodisiac. Love works at any age, with any two people, at any time of day or night.

April

April in Paris. Or Chicago. Or New York, Boston, or Oshkosh. Or the suburbs of any city in any state. So lovely for lovers. You can take a walk in the rain, you can gather tulips and daffodils for each other. The promise of warmer days and even warmer nights brings lovers close. Sometimes, just holding hands as you walk down a drizzly street at twilight is the best. Sometimes, it's hiding under the covers with a flashlight talking about anything and nothing.

Steamy looks are provocative, but talk is what brings us together. When we really care about another person, we can drop the mask and open the floodgates of feeling. Take a deep breath, sigh a little, and communicate. Your love will grow as you become more expressive—with words and without.

Communication

Couples who "never talk anymore" typically never have sex anymore either. Their topics are: the house, the kids, the car— and that's it. Why should their romantic life be any richer? If you want to get along in bed, you have to be able to express yourself. Get closer by talking about your emotions, opinions, ideas, hopes, and fears. Then you'll find you really have something to say to one another in bed and out of bed.

How To Get Through To Your Partner

One. **Be an empathic listener.** If you pay attention to the one you love, you are giving and getting at the same time. Your lover feels accepted and understood; you get to be a part of what he or she is going through.

Two. **Be direct.** When you want support, adoration, a change in the relationship, or anything else—say what you really feel. Give more than a clue—reveal yourself.

Three. **Match your words and gestures.** Make sure your verbal and nonverbal communication is in sync. If you say you're in the mood for love, but pull away from a hug, you're giving a mixed message.

Four. *Use descriptive language.* The more vivid your words, the easier you are to understand. Say, "When you kiss my eyelids, I feel your tenderness toward me," instead of the generic, "I love the way you kiss."

Five. *Talk about sex together.* Exchange information about your needs, desires, wishes, secrets and fantasies. Then ask questions. Maybe you want to know if your spouse of twenty years has ever wanted to have sex in a tent in the backyard. Maybe he wants to know if you'd like to make love in the back row of a movie theater. Finally, ask for what you want—but ask nicely. Maybe some of your dreams will coincide. Even if they don't, they may stimulate some new ideas that you do wish to share.

Wonderful Nonverbal Ways to Let Your Partner Know What You Want

One. Sigh softly when it feels good.

Two. Moan when it feels even better.

Three. Gently move your hands to where you want your partner's hands to be.

Four. Show him how to stroke your skin by doing it yourself.

Five. Write a graphic love note.

Six. Dance together when you're overwhelmed with delight.

Attitudes for Romantic Sex

*T*he power of positive thinking can get you through anything. A positive

attitude lifts you up—and inspires all those close to you. Think to yourself,

"I feel special and desirable" every time you're around your partner. See whether

you don't get admiring glances and melting sighs of passion.

The Best Attitudes for Romantic Sex

One. **Knowledge.** Learn everything you can about your partner's desires—and your own.

Two. **Courage.** Good sexual simpatico takes a little courage. Take a deep breath and ask for the kind of loving you crave.

Three. **Freedom.** Lovemaking is about "wants," not "shoulds." Go with what your true nature demands.

Four. *Trust.* The best sex happens when two people feel safe enough to be vulnerable with one another.

Five. *Generosity.* When you give romantically, you get back threefold what you've extended to your lover.

Six. *Humor.* Sex can be fun, and funny, too. Couples who can laugh at themselves can really enjoy each other.

May

*M*ay is a month to be mad and wild and throw away inhibition. Sleep under the stars on the first warm night. Zip your sleeping bags together, set up a tent in the backyard and make the rest of the world disappear. Smell the crisp air; feel the breeze wafting through overhanging boughs.

Maybe you'd like to launch a rowboat in a sheltered pond one calm night and lie down together in it and watch the stars, drifting wherever the current takes you.

Maybe you could rent a bicycle built for two and ride the length of your home town, stopping at an ice cream stand on the way home to share licks of a chocolate fudge swirl cone.

Anything is possible now that the weather has turned. Love is more than in the air—it's inside you.

$\mathscr{S}exual\ \mathscr{P}ick\text{-}\mathscr{M}e\text{-}\mathscr{U}ps$

One. Play a game of strip Monopoly™.

Two. Unplug the TV and spend the evening talking.

Three. Dance naked by candlelight.

Four. Make love without hands.

Five. Give your partner a pedicure.

Six. Write each other an erotic poem.

Seven. Sneak off to the kitchen to kiss during dinner at your parents' house.

Eight. Schedule a rendezvous in the backseat of your car.

Nine. Have a picnic in bed—Chinese takeout, wine, and scented candles.

Joybreak: Celebrate May Day

Get up with the sun and savor the quiet hour before the world wakes up. No cars, no phones ringing, just the two of you taking a walk in the morning dew.

Like Joe and Nancy, you can have a breakfast picnic in a field when the dew is still on the grass. They brought fruit and croissants and a big thermos of coffee. As they sat and let the sun warm their faces, they watched two new fawns dance out of the woods, coming close and then gamboling away.

"I love it here. I don't want to leave," he told her.

"We don't have to. Let's fool around all day."

They hugged, touching bodies from the top of their heads to the ankles. "Do you think anyone else in the world has ever felt this way?"

"How do you feel?" he asked.

"Drunk on you, and the day."

Slowly, they ate their meal, kissing in between bites. They watched the sun rise in the sky and searched for four-leaf clovers. But they already had all the luck they needed. They had each other.

June

$\mathcal{I}$t is time to make promises and then keep them. June is a month to marry, or to dance sensuously at your friends' wedding and make them incredibly jealous as you kiss on the dance floor and everyone asks, "Who are they and how did they get so happy?"

Think about your own commitment to each other. Have you been together for years and years? Maybe a rededication of your vows is in order. Have you just decided to become a couple? All the more reason to rejoice about the bond that now ties you.

$\mathscr{I}ntimacy$

$\mathscr{M}$en and women long to be joined together—but so much keeps us apart. Truly, we crave closeness, caring, and mutual nurturing. When sex occurs in such a connected relationship, it is psychologically, emotionally, and spiritually the most satisfying thing on earth.

It's scary but wonderful to feel so close that your hearts beat in time and you can finish each others' sentences.

How to Get Intimate

One. *Accept your partner as he or she is.* Don't try and change what's there—just enjoy it, laugh at it, understand it.

Two. *Acknowledge his reluctance—and sometimes yours—to be intimate.* Intimacy requires you to open up to your lover as you do to no one else. That takes some risk. But the risk is worth it if you are both willing to be vulnerable.

Three. *Recognize that change takes time.* You can't get that close overnight. But the time you spend coming together is part of the joy in this relationship.

Sexy Hints For Couples

You can take intimacy a step further when you join forces sexually. The better you know each other, the more you will please each other.

One. **Become more self-indulgent.** Enjoy every pleasure you've got, from a long, hot bath to an afternoon at the movies. Luxuriate in small delights.

Two. **Schedule one hour a week for just the two of you.** Maybe you'll choose to make love or take a long walk or lie in each other's arms in front of the fireplace. No pressure.

Three. *Give each other a ten-minute massage.* The one getting the gift picks the area to be massaged.

Four. *Jump into bed together.* For sleeping, that is. Try to coordinate your bedtimes whenever you can. Snuggling and spooning is nice in every season.

Five. *Set your clock for midnight love.* Have a date in the middle of the night, when the rest of the world is asleep.

Six. *Play like children.* Pretend for the night that you are characters from a favorite book, film, or fairy tale. A new role can set your libido free.

JOYBREAK: MOTHER'S AND FATHER'S DAY—ROMANCE FOR PARENTS

Remember the days before kids when you could leave your bedroom door open? When you could prepare a love-feast in the kitchen naked and enjoy feeding each other sweet treats at any time of day or night? Today's the day to recapture the luxury of being temporarily childless and in love.

You can celebrate being a mother and father by enlisting your own parents or some friends to take your children for a day and an evening. Pretend you've just met and are going on your first date—see a movie and share a soda as you shyly get to know each other. Or perhaps you want to acknowledge how much has passed between you over the years. In that case, go and rent a hotel room (even a no-tell motel on the highway can be deliciously naughty and nice) or use your own house where you can relish the sound of your lover's voice with no overlay of childish chatter. Forget the chores; do only fun things. Water the garden together and spray each other with the hose; play touch football in the grass and tackle your partner all you can. Give your love a gift of satin sheets and roll around on them all night.

This is your time—just the two of you. No responsibilities, no obligations to anyone other than the person you're crazy about.

July

$\mathcal{P}$assion is hot and parched. There's no way to quench the thirst you have for your lover, and you are drenched with the juices that run off you whenever you even think of him. You sense the heat of the earth rising up toward you, and you match it with your own. There is a heaviness to all your movements—when you touch, you stick together. It's impossible to keep your cool—but who wants to now?

In the summer, you are acutely aware of the sounds around you—the cooing of birds, the click of the cicadas, the hum of air conditioners. Your own lovemaking can be sensitized and heightened when you add sound to it.

Aural Arousal

*M*usic appeals to the senses by evoking feelings—passion, tenderness, anticipation. Lovemaking is more exciting with a sound track, too.

You can seduce your lover with music—light classical, funky blues, hot jazz, or something ephemeral and New Age-y. Keep the stereo on while you make love, too. And then *you* can take over. Nearly everyone is aroused by the sounds of lovemaking—sex has a language all its own.

Six Hints for Erotic Expression

One. **Pant, groan, and moan.** Throw yourself into your lovemaking and let yourself go. The more vocal you are, the more you excite each other.

Two. **Learn the art of hot talk.** Talk about what you want or what you're going to do together. Be juicy and specific.

Three. **Make eye contact.** It increases the impact of your words and sounds.

Four. **After lovemaking, keep talking.** You can whisper about anything that keeps you close and cuddling—what to do this summer, great movies, a perfect sunset you saw together last week.

JOYBREAK: THE FOURTH OF JULY

It's a day for fireworks—but you don't need a town permit to set off the ones you have in mind.

The day passes in a hot, languid haze, and when evening comes, you drive toward a park outside of town. When he parks the car, you reach over to stroke his cheek. "I love everything about you," he says.

In the background, you can hear a rumble, then a pop. The sky is suddenly alight with brilliant blazes—a white cloud of stars, a green palm tree, a blue umbrella that suddenly turns red, then dribbles out of the sky.

"Just like us," he says, "explosive."

You climb into the backseat and roll down the window. Curled up together, you watch the night sky turn every color of the rainbow. Then you turn to each other—and the colors seem even brighter. Each kiss, each caress, feels like the breeze through the open window.

Tomorrow seems as far away as the moon.

August

Be teenagers for a day. Get giddy on an amusement park ride and clutch each other, screaming. Don't think about anything serious; just have a grand old time.

Every once in a while, pretend you just met. That way, you have beginner's mind about what attracted you in the first place. Look at your lover carefully—admire the eyelashes, the walk, the sound of that dear voice. Now there's a person you could go for . . . and do.

Flirting

Flirting is fun. It's a teasing, easy way to tell another person you're interested. Where's the harm in letting someone know they're attractive and appreciated, with no demands or expectations stated or implied? Flirtation is nothing more than that. It may lead to a date or a relationship, or can renew the excited feelings you had when you first met. Flirting broadcasts your sexuality on the right channel.

Rules of Flirting

One. **Make eye contact while you flirt.** How you look at someone says a lot about your intention.

Two. **Keep your comments lighthearted.** Flirting should be delicious, fun and safe for everyone, even the very married.

Three. **Use touch sparingly.** Touch the other person's hand or arm every once in a while to emphasize a point. In advanced flirting, run a finger down the other person's cheek.

Four. **Be subtle.** Hold her gaze a moment longer than necessary. Lower your voice when you talk to a man in a crowded room so he'll have to lean forward to catch your words.

$\mathcal{I}$f you've flirted successfully, you will be itching to connect physically. You'll want to get in close and personal, to nudge and tickle and giggle about those secret, private things you share. Sometimes, you want to get sexy in ways that you usually wouldn't consider romantic, just to say you'd done it.

Lovebites

*M*outh-watering. Sexplay as a luscious meal. More a gentle nibble than a true bite, this form of erotic enticement was so practiced in ancient times that the Hindu erotic writers composed lengthy lists of where and how hard to "bite." This is a stimulating activity that can perk up any relationship when done right. And love-biting will make you feel like kids again, parking at the drive-in, fooling around.

The Best Spots For Lovebites

One. **Ears.** Nibble the fleshy lobes. Then run your tongue inside the ear.

Two. **Neck.** Nibble and suck the neck (remember "hickeys"?), and don't forget the nape.

Three. **Fingers and toes.** Don't neglect your sweetie's extremities. Suck. Occasionally take a small nibble. Enjoy!

Joybreak: A Summer Luncheon

Why not go home for lunch? It's summer, it's slow—nothing much going on at the office. Call your partner at about 10:30 with a promise of something better than a sandwich.

Set the table with fine china and damask napkins and serve grapes, cucumbers in dill sauce, and finely sliced ham. When he comes in, the music should be playing, the iced tea poured. Be formal with each other, tentative and a little awkward. Sit down across the table and watch the sunshine spill on your bodies, etching you in light. While you eat, slip off a shoe and surreptitiously wind your foot up inside his pant leg.

Soon you will feel an ache so deep, you have to touch. Place a grape in your mouth and come across the table to him. During your kiss, transfer the grape, mouth to mouth. See where that leads. Maybe you'll stay right where you are, dropping to the floor to embrace; maybe you'll follow a trail of breadcrumbs to the bedroom upstairs.

Take your time, spin out the lunch hour as long as you possibly can. You may not remember anything you ate, but the day will be memorable.

September

$\mathcal{Q}$uestionnaire

$\mathcal{T}$here are no right or wrong answers. This is simply a quiz for you and your partner to take separately, then together. Your answers should tell you what each finds satisfying or dissatisfying in your relationship and give you the chance to make a few exciting changes.

Put aside an evening when you have several uninterrupted hours to spend together. Snuggle up on the couch, relax, and see where your answers lead.

Questions to Deepen Your Relationship

One. How often do you hold each other and feel close without being sexual?

Two. How often do you make love?

Three. Do you and your partner show or tell each other how you want to be touched, stroked, kissed, and caressed?

Four. What three elements of your relationship do you enjoy most?

Five. What are your top three suggestions for heating the fire between you and your partner?

Six. What could you do to strengthen your relationship?

Seven. What could you do for your partner outside the bedroom that would have a good effect on your sex life?

Eight. Name your partner's secret places, the spots where he or she is most sensitive to touch.

Nine. What does your partner do to arouse you?

Ten. What's the most romantic thing you've ever done together?

Joybreak: Bedroom School Days

It's always nice to learn a new skill. Who says you can't teach old lovers new tricks? What about a video tape to let the experts give you pointers on spicy lovemaking?

Two Eastern practices can help you prolong and intensify your lovemaking and achieve a closer, more spiritual union. Taoism (from China) and Tantrism (from India) take the emphasis off physical sexuality so that the spirit can rise.

There are wonderful maneuvers any couple can learn to make sex more rewarding. Pleasure-oriented rather than goal-oriented, this type of lovemaking has one underlying principle: let arousal build slowly. Pay more attention to the steam coming from the pot than the fire underneath it.

Eastern Sex Techniques Any Couple Can Use

One. **Deep breathing.** Let air fill your chest cavity and expand it, then slowly exhale. Lie in spoon position with your partner. Imagine you have a nose on your chest and are breathing your partner into your body as you take deep breaths. Reverse positions.

Next, face each other, close your eyes, and synchronize your breathing together. You inhale, your partner exhales—as though it were the same breath.

Two. **The eye lock.** Keep your eyes open during lovemaking. You'll be surprised as you hold each others gaze how this intensifies your passion for each other.

*Three. **Lift your spirit.*** Imagine that the two of you have become One. You are no longer individuals with flesh-and-blood bodies, but one soaring spirit.

*Four. **Take your time.*** You don't have to go anywhere, or reach any peak. You have no goal, no intention other than relishing each other's company.

*Five. **Let joy expand in your heart.*** You are blessed because you belong together.

October

$\mathcal{T}$he leaves swirl and settle into pools of gold, crimson, and orange. The smell of woodsmoke brings you inside again, and even when you're apart, you can feel each other's presence.

It's delightful to imagine your lover when you're alone. You can see the person exactly as she is, or change her slightly to make her even more appealing to your libido. You can twist and turn your emotions and interests any way you like. The brain is the most influential sex organ we've got— so use it to the fullest.

Fantasy

Fantasy is a mental aphrodisiac. Sometimes it's a conscious process; sometimes not. You can fantasize about making love in an elevator that's stuck around the forty-ninth floor, or you can conjure up a fleeting thought about your partner—great eyes, great hair, great hands—that turns you on.

The kisses you share begin in your imagination, bringing a lurch to the pit of your stomach. You can picture your faces coming closer; you can feel the touch without touch. And then, when you actually press flesh to flesh, it feels more vivid, more enticing than ever.

Your fantasies don't have to be sexual wishes that you want to come true. As a matter of fact, it's better to keep them as whims, wild thoughts that you need not tame in your mind. The mysterious nature of these waking dreams is what keeps them ever fresh and delicious.

After you've had time to think about exactly what you'd like to do, get together and do it. Use the impetus of your fantasy life to drive your desire over the edge. Sex is miraculous whether it's fast or slow. We can do it so many ways and fulfill so many different fantasies. One way that keeps a romantic spark alive is the "quickie." There's no real time for making love, so instead you go with the spontaneous combustion between two people.

Top Sexual Fantasies

One. Making love with someone you've always secretly had a yen for.

Two. A romantic idyll—sex on a beach or in a cabin in the woods.

Three. A spontaneous encounter where strangers meet and are at once on fire—their clothes drop away as they melt into each others' arms.

Four. Being watched while making love.

Five. Sex with a celebrity.

$\mathcal{Q}uickies$

$\mathcal{A}$ "quickie" is a brief episode of lovemaking that takes you from ground zero to infinity in just a few moments of ecstasy. The urgency and excitement inherent in the encounter can make it a stimulating and pleasurable experience for both partners.

In the best of all possible quickies, a man and a woman look at each other and ignite. They come together at the boiling point and seize the moment.

A few minutes of passion can act as a jolt of sexual caffeine into the bloodstream of your relationship.

The Golden Rules of Quickies

One. *Use as a sometime thing—not all the time.* Every once in a while, they put you right in the moment. You just don't want them to become the norm in your relationship.

Two. *Be open to erotic opportunity.* No time to make love until the weekend comes? Slip into the bathroom together for those few minutes the children are engrossed in "Sesame Street." Don't overlook any sexual possibility.

Three. *If there's time and energy for something more, let it happen.* Maybe you meant it to be a quickie so you could both get back to work, but it feels too nice and you're too engrossed to stop. Fine! Put aside the rest of your life occasionally so you can really enjoy each other.

JOYBREAK: HALLOWEEN

All Hallows Eve means dressing up in costumes to fulfill each other's fantasies. This is a time of year when spirits run amuck, ghosts are in the air, and you can be a truly free soul, roving the earth. This is a perfect holiday to turn yourself inside out, and make your relationship into something you didn't think you were capable of.

Sexual Energizers

One. **Look the way you feel.** Select sensuous, sensual clothing, styles and colors that flatter you and make you feel desirable. A costume can be the image of what you'd like to be, or what you think will turn on your lover. If you can dress for success, you can dress for sex, too.

Two. *Get in shape together.* You feel sexier when you're in good physical condition—strong and flexible and filled with endurance. It's energizing to exercise with your lover—and this prepares you for bedroom activities.

Three. *Write sexy letters.* Correspond erotically with your partner, even if you live together—the letters will be a turn on for the writer and the reader. You can also borrow someone else's words and adapt them. Use sexy novels and poems as inspiration.

Four. *Create romantic rituals.* Send flowers on Halloween—great big yellow mums or one red, waxy anthurium with its tongue sticking out. Give affection—with your voice, eyes, hands, and every part of you. Plan dates and mini-vacations as often as you can afford them. Create ceremonies that would mean nothing to anyone but the two of you—they are powerful ways of reconnecting with those feelings of attraction and passion that first moved you.

Five. Step out of role. Be someone you're not. Increase your romantic range by "reversing" roles with your partner. Sometimes, you be the leader and let your lover be the follower. Then switch.

November

$\mathcal{T}$he year is nearly done, but you have just begun. A time of the year, when you want to roam from one antique shop to another, pretending you are incredibly rich and can have the most outrageous things in the store. The window-shopping is just as much fun as the real thing, because you're imagining yet another part of the extraordinary life that you share.

This is a perfect month to go to the beach because no one's there. You stroll the dunes hand in hand, listening to the ocean's roar. Except for a few fishermen, and a girl riding a horse out of the mists, there is no one on the beach but you and the one you love. You can get sand in your shoes and collect shells and stock up on memories that will last you a lifetime.

Sensuality

The most romantic among us knows his lover's mind and body like the back of his hand. He knows her smell, her taste, the way she looks in a certain light, the sound of her voice and the insistent press of her fingers in his clasp. When you explore your senses, the delight you feel in your partner expands infinitely.

Good lovers are also sensual people. Each day, they awaken to new sights, sounds, smells, tastes, and touches. The intricacies of how you and your lover delight in those five and of course, the sixth sense—intuition—says a lot about your relationship. Rev up your senses and your sexuality will expand.

Think about tasting your lover's lips: the incredible kisses, the slightly salty forearms, the sweetness of delectable fingers.

Think about the scent that permeates his skin and body—you can enhance it with perfumes, massage oils, scented candles, flowers, and the seductive aroma of special foods you can take into the bedroom with you.

Think about seeing your lover for the first time every time you get up in the morning.

Think about hearing that beloved voice on the phone, or when she's just down the street and calls your name.

Think about sliding skin on skin—goosebumps may rise the minute you make contact.

Exercises to Awaken Sensuality

One. **The sensory surprise.** Take turns planning a lovemaking session with emphasis on the sensory delights. One of you may prepare a bedroom feast, the other spray the room with rosewater and put rose petals on the bed. Add some detail that will stimulate each of your senses.

Two. **Touch focusing.** Close your eyes and use only your sense of touch. Run your hands over your lover's skin and note how the texture changes from place to place.

Three. ***Touch expanding.*** Use fabrics and temperature-changers in your lovemaking—lie on leather, run velvet on your limbs; try fur, silk, feathers, warm water, ice.

Four. ***Sound play.*** Put excitement into your pillow talk. Talk "dirty." Have phone sex. Sing to each other.

Five. ***Awareness expansion.*** Take your sensory awareness out of the bedroom. Take a walk in a place you know but this time, examine the trees. Go to the supermarket and only buy red things.

The Weekend Getaway

To raise your romance to a fever pitch, get away from the everyday.
Go somewhere where no one knows you. Register at a hotel and use a foreign
accent; eat foods you've never tried; make up a silly story about where you came
from. Be one another's confidant and pal here in this different place.

You need to get away, so you rent a cabin with a jacuzzi and a fireplace, far from everything and everyone.

Don't tell him what the destination is—just pack and go. You stop for dinner at an Italian restaurant right off the road. To his persistent question, "but where are we going?" you give an enigmatic smile. You order your meals as a pianist begins to play and a few diners take their places on the tiny dance floor.

He takes your hand and leads you to the center of the floor. Every pore, every cell is attached to him in some way. He holds you so close, you can't tell where he begins and you end.

"Let's get out of here," he whispers in your ear. "I bet you've got great plans for tonight."

You ask for the dinners to be wrapped and take off like a shot down the road. By the time you get to the cabin you're both laughing hysterically. "A romance emergency; gotta split," you giggle.

The full moon lights your path to the cabin—now it's getting chilly. "Where in the world are we?" he asks.

"Nowhere," you say. "We're out of the world." You wrap your arms around each other, deciding to bring in the luggage later. The lights flicker when you turn them on, so you opt for candles all over the room. For a moment, you just stand in the doorway, breathing in the night air. The stillness is overwhelming.

Lead him by the hand to the jacuzzi on the outside deck. "Too cold," he protests.

"Not once we're in." You turn on the water and the jets.

Quickly shedding your clothes, you put on the plush terrycloth robes parked on the back of the door. You step outside and drop the robes. Both of you are outlined in moonlight—there is a silvery cast to your hair and limbs. You shiver a little and step into the warm bubbles. Settling in, you sit thigh to thigh and kiss. Your kisses are long and torturous; to break them up, you push off into the center of the tub and float, body to body. The hum of the jacuzzi is the only accompaniment to your slow, sensuous water dance.

Joybreak: A Thanksgiving Day Feast

The family ate hearty—and a good time was had by all. After the last relatives left, Pam closed the door and snuck up behind Phil, grabbing him around the waist. "I thought they'd never leave."

He stretched his arms back and turned in her embrace. The kitchen was strewn with plates and leftovers. "Just leave this mess; I'll take care of it in the morning."

Pam grinned at him, taking a chuck of cranberry in her mouth. "I don't know, I didn't eat a whole lot—I was serving the whole time." She leaned in for a kiss, and let the cranberry sauce flow from her lips to his. "How about you?"

"I could eat again," he said, licking his lips and looking at her lasciviously. "If you were my platter."

There was a bowl of leftover mashed potatoes, still slightly warm, as was the turkey gravy. Phil knelt before her and put a dollop on her bare knee.

"You wouldn't dare. It's . . . un-American to do this on Thanksgiving."

"But I love you. You look like a Norman Rockwell painting in that prim and proper dress," he says. "I swear I'm patriotic." He licked the potatoes off her knee, then, when he felt her shiver, he offered her the bowl.

"I give thanks for every day we're together," she whispered, as she unbuttoned his shirt and put some potato in the recess made by his clavicle. "Yum."

It was the perfect holiday meal.

December

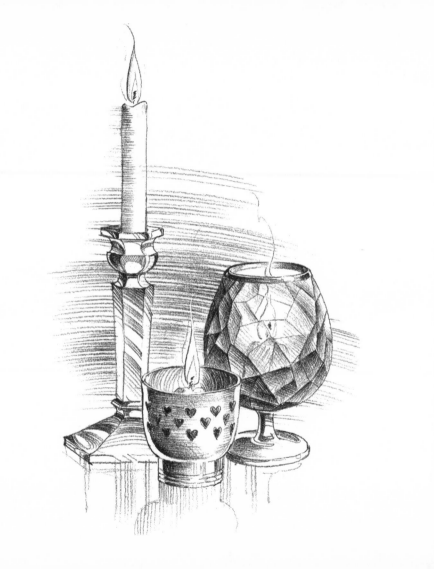

*G*ifts that weren't bought in stores are best for lovers. You want to give of yourself, and each offering should be a token of love. It may be a branch of holly to put over the headboard, or a swirl of fresh snow that you race in from the cold and douse with maple syrup as a treat. Each of you take an evening to give to the other: prepare a luscious meal, give a massage with scented oil, turn down the bedsheets. Doing for each other with no thought of yourself is what creates the feeling that each day, in each season, you are growing closer—respecting each other's differences but celebrating the fact that you two are one.

The piney scent of the Christmas tree reminds you to keep your love fresh and true. One particularly nice gift that costs nothing is an erotic massage. You can while away the hours touching—without being sexual—getting drunk on the pleasures of touch.

An Erotic Massage

*Y*ou want to caress, fondle, cuddle, and work out the kinks in tight muscles and joints. You want to take time to explore the landscape of your lover's body—discover those unique places that fill you with rapture. This type of physical contact is different from sex—it is pure sensual experience.

There is a hunger for body contact within all of us, and good touching is often neglected even in the closest relationships. We don't have to be about to engage in sexual activity to put hand to leg, shoulder to back, or forehead to neck.

Giving an Erotic Massage

One. Start with your clothes on. Let your hands lightly brush your lover's limbs. Every once in a while, reach under a shirt sleeve or up a pant leg to give an intimation of what's coming next.

Two. Now you can help your partner undress. Warm a little baby oil or lotion in your hands and lightly massage your partner all over, starting with the back and working with a combination of the following strokes:

♥ *Gliding.* Let your hands glide smoothly over the surface of your partner's body. Make long strokes flow into each other.

♥ *Kneading.* Relieve tension and arouse your partner at the same time. Think of a cat, kneading her velvet paws into soft skin.

♥ *Spider walking.* Use your fingerpads as lightly as if they were spider legs and walk all over your partner's body. Barely touch the surface of the skin.

Three. Use your hair, mouth, breasts, and other body parts to stroke your partner.

Four. Massage the buttocks, first kneading, then teasing. Talk to your partner about how his body feels in your hands.

Five. Do the front side next. Start at the top, paying close attention to the forehead, eyes, ears, and mouth. Work your fingers into the neck. Make slow trips up the arms, then up the legs, across the belly, ending at the chest.

Six. Kiss the heart and feel it beat under your hand. Stay quiet together for a few moments; then switch places.

You will find that desire floods both of you as you gently but firmly touch the body in this penetrating way.

JOYBREAK: HOLIDAY SEASON

It would be fun to be Santa; it would be fun to be a present. Dress up in plastic wrap, then put on real clothes. Maybe something unbelievably dull, like long underwear and a bulky sweater, maybe something fun like a tablecloth or the drapes. On top of these, you'll need a blanket. Walk toward your lover, flashing a little of what's underneath. Let him take you into the hallway and roll you into a throw rug.

When you're immobilized and can't do a thing, he can shower you with tinsel you didn't use on the tree, then kiss the excess silver strands out of your eyes, cheeks, and mouth.

Now it's time for him to unwrap you. He'll start with the rug, rolling you gently back and forth, making you wriggle as you emerge from your cocoon.

Let him unwrap the blanket, taking his time as he exposes your feet, your legs, your torso and arms. Don't be surprised when he kisses and fondles each part of you, his excitement rising as he sees your familiar form reappearing.

He will strip off the sweater and run his hand the length of you, watching the expression on your face. Then he'll help you pull off the underwear and draw you close to the tree. As he spins you out of the plastic wrap and peels you gently, he says, "You are the best present I ever had. The gift that keeps on giving."

You can see in his eyes how adored you are. Christmas is such a joyous time to share.

Other Special Days for Lovers

*W*hen you create a special ceremony to share with the one you love, you give your life shape and substance. Whether it's a national holiday that you've embellished with certain unique touches, or an occasion you've concocted all by yourself, commemorating a special day is emotionally invigorating.

You and your lover can come up with your own exceptional rituals, setting the scene for beautiful memories. You'll be able to look back as you look forward, remembering the birthday when you went fishing at midnight or the anniversary where you got locked in the library and had to sleep in the stacks.

Anything you do together makes a moment that's all yours. It will be forever inscribed for you in the book of life.

A Romantic Birthday Party

What do you need for a romantic birthday party? The ingredients are:

♥ ice cream

♥ balloons

♥ a simple gift—maybe some silk underwear or a set of wooden windchimes

♥ silly hats

♥ a tape recorder

♥ plenty of towels

♥ pictures of the two of you as babies, pasted on a birthday card to look as though you were together even then

♥ two tickets in a sleeper car on a train, going wherever your heart desires.

Let the train staff know in advance that you do not wish to be disturbed and you will make up your berths yourselves.

Make a tape—maybe a few old friends wishing your lover the very best, a silly poem from you, a love sonnet written by a master that you've read with meaning and affection.

As the train pulls out of the station, blow up your balloons, put on your hats, and open the card and the present. After kissing for a while, pull down the shades and open your hamper, which contains a particularly rich ice cream cake. As you speed along into the night, you can feed each other cake with your fingers or take off your clothes and have a love banquet right there in the train car. (Keep the towels handy!)

When the party is over, wash off and make up the bed. Climb into the upper berth together. Let the rhythm of the train rock you to sleep in each other's arms.

Anniversary to Rededicate Your Passion

*H*ow long have you been together? It gets harder to remember as the years pass. There have been great times, lean times, times when you wanted to run away from home, times of acute boredom, times of strife and anger, and times when there was nothing as wonderful as coming home at the end of a long day to the arms of the one person on earth who understood.

All that—and more—can be included in your anniversary celebration.

Begin the day with a remembrance of that long-ago proposal. Did you get down on your knees, did you present a ring while on a roller coaster, or was it a more casual discussion that led to a mutual decision to marry? Do it again—but this time, substitute new words that have come to mean something to you as your love has grown from infancy to maturity.

Next, go to a sun-filled room and make love. This is a day to consecrate the way you touch—you two have your own connection, your own language, your own way of coming together in ecstasy.

Then, give each other a bath to cleanse body and spirit. Each partner can wash the other's hair and give the one they love a soapy massage that works on every sore muscle and every old tension.

Next, select special clothing. You can dress in the same color or fabric to announce your coupledom. Dress for the weather, but add a touch to your ensemble that symbolizes each season to show the eternity of your love.

Now pick a place (perhaps the place you first met, or a location that has come to mean a lot to you over the years), and spend several hours making up a new ritual—something that combines your personalities, your senses of humor, and your hopes for the future.

When you're hungry, go out for a lovely meal. It doesn't have to be fancy, but you'll want to eat your favorite foods. Candles and wine are appropriate, but what's more important is having a small, crowded table so that your bodies have to touch at all times.

At the end of the day, drive to a secluded spot to watch the moon rise. Look into each other's eyes and see what you first saw in each other—the passion, the desire, the fun, the romance, the dear face you know as well as your own. Make a date for the same time next year.

Finale

We all want to get closer. That urge to merge with another is instinctive, and when we've found the right one, there's nothing we'd rather do than be with the one we love.

Romance comes in many shapes and sizes—sometimes it has the intensity of great opera; at other times, it's as light as a sunfish on the water. When it's present, though, you can abandon all other thoughts and activities. You have to seize these precious moments and make them your own. Sometimes you have to make them up out of whole cloth—but with a good imagination and a willing partner, you'll never run out of opportunities.

For example: Disguise yourself as a pirate and offer your love a new land you've just conquered; make like an animal and find a refuge for the two of you in the woods. Think about love when you are mowing the lawn, washing the car, preparing a meal. It covers you like a warm blanket and dresses you in the clear light of irrational joy.

Find pleasure with each other every moment of every day. Be bold, be sexy, be sweet, and always remember the old-fashioned things like hearts and flowers that never go out of style.

You will be the kind of lover you were meant to be—the one who is most valued, cherished, and desired.